LEARNING IN LANGUAGE
AND LITERATURE

THE BURTON LECTURE

THE INGLIS LECTURE

1962

LEARNING IN LANGUAGE
AND LITERATURE

Insistent Tasks in Language Learning

A. R. MacKINNON

The Developing Imagination

NORTHROP FRYE

DISTRIBUTED FOR THE

GRADUATE SCHOOL OF EDUCATION

OF HARVARD UNIVERSITY BY

Harvard University Press

CAMBRIDGE, MASSACHUSETTS

1963

Contents

Contents

THE BURTON LECTURE

Insistent Tasks in Language Learning

A. R. MacKINNON

THE BURTON LECTURESHIP

In order to stimulate interest and research in elementary education, Dr. and Mrs. William H. Burton gave to the Graduate School of Education, Harvard University, a fund for the maintenance of a lectureship under which a distinguished scholar or leader would be invited each year to discuss national problems in this field. Dr. Burton, who was Director of Apprenticeship at Harvard for sixteen years, has taught for forty-six years in the fields of elementary education and teacher education.

Insistent Tasks in Language Learning

A. R. MacKINNON

Language learning, whether English, Spanish, French, or Russian, is not something that just happens; it is something that has been brought about by persons in communion with other persons. The intellectual and emotional processes whereby the feat is accomplished are exceedingly delicate, complex, and persistent; learning which takes place at early stages is inextricably bound up with all later stages in myriad ways.

Such elementary facts of language learning should be automatically assumed in practice by persons engaged in bringing about learning in our schools. Yet an intensive study of the thousands of articles written on the topic reveals little unanimity in the aims and practices employed. Some writers evaluate language learning solely on the basis of what can be measured by scores on objective tests without regard for the ways the measurable products of learning were attained (or whether they should ever have been attained in the first place). Others regard the human mind as if it were some plastic material to be molded into some prescribed shape, or a muscle which must be put through its paces on a mental gymnasium every so often, or a dull instrument which must be sharpened up in the present for later use. Acknowledgment is made frequently of stages in development, but an amazing number of assumptions are tacitly made about what has happened before a particular stage and what is to follow. Brooks suggests that the greater part of the writing about teaching language can be "dismissed as irrelevant once it is granted that this teaching is to be appraised in terms of the learning that is to be presumed to be its concomitant. For the fact that a great deal of animated and well-disposed teaching takes place, accompanied even by lively and well-intentioned study, is no assurance that any significant degree of learning will result." [1]

Even the "articulated English program" proposed by the Modern Language Association in 1959 is still little more than a "hypothesis to test." The hope of persons advancing the program is that "the subject 'English' will again emerge from the educational system of the United States together with the humanistic values it has traditionally but, heretofore, vaguely held. Now almost anything goes into English courses." [2]

The frankness of the Modern Language Association is timely in the face of mounting evidence that the lack of a connected, over-all view of language learning may be taking a frightening toll in persons' mental lives. Watt, writing as early as 1944, voiced the fears of many persons concerned with language instruction when he stated: "The

4

results of our systematic instruction over a period of nine years of child life during the past half-century have not been altogether satisfying; indeed, there is ground for the fear that we may be training the vast majority of our children just well enough to enable them to occupy themselves with the tawdriest reading material and yet not well enough to ensure that they will wish to enter into and enjoy their rightful intellectual and spiritual heritage or even that they will be able to withstand the word-magic of the advertiser and that of the propagandist." [3]

A growing volume of studies, plus increased public criticism, indicate that Watt's fears were not unfounded. Black's study of college students[4] is simply one example of the documentation taking place. He found that misunderstanding of what was read was frequent. Often there was failure to understand the author's general argument and the conclusion which he drew. Key words were frequently misunderstood, especially when quite common words were used to express uncommon or abstract ideas. Even when the students understood the "meanings" of words in isolation, they still could not manage to grasp the argument and the intention of the writer.

The fact that Mickey Spillane's books can be best sellers is little comfort for those who maintain that with modern methods of teaching reading more pupils are reading than ever before. The school dropout frequently exhibits language helplessness; the juvenile delinquent is often the retarded reader in school and the child having difficulty in problem solving in mathematics is found to be struggling not only with mathematics but also with the vagaries of the English language.[5]

Few primary-grade teachers have any understanding of the work of secondary-school English teachers outside of their own dim recollections of what took place when they were in secondary school. The secondary-school teacher, in turn, tends either to view with alarm the "modern" practices of teaching language in the elementary school and to insist that more literary quality should be imposed on the learning or, in the face of his own feelings of hopelessness, he views with undeserved praise the work of the first-grade teacher, for she has at least managed to teach the pupils *something* when they learn to read. And the university person tends to regard both primary and secondary schools as primarily the training ground for "the really important work" in language.

In the light of such fragmented thinking about language learning, it is not surprising that graduate students understand remarkably little of what they read. What should engender more surprise is that they understand as much as they do.

The fragmentation has had its repercussions beyond the range of language learning; it has increased the gulf between the literary "intellectuals" and the scientists. C. P. Snow writes: "Thirty years ago the cultures had long ceased to speak to each other: but at least they managed a kind of frozen smile across the gulf. Now the politeness has gone, and they just make faces." [6] The hiatus is real enough in adults' thinking; it is growing increasingly among pupils at school.

The gulf is certainly the product of multiple causation, but teachers must share a considerable portion of the blame through their failure to give to their students any adequate realization that science and poetry are both equally born of the imagination. There can be no doubt that all significant achievements in science as well as in art are the expression of human imaginative power—that same power from which language springs.

The implicit plea here for a synoptic view of the various branches of learning is only too familiar; there are literally thousands of attempts being made to bridge the gap between the two cultures. Survey courses in English literature and science proliferate at the university level and humanistic and scientific eclecticism predominate in the selection of curricula for the elementary and secondary school. It is exceedingly difficult to find evidence that the attempts have succeeded in giving the pupils an appreciation of the modes of thought and feeling through which the various arts and sciences are advanced, and of the nature of the common humanity which is active in these diverse forms of experience. The outcomes are more frequently a crystallization of a student's attitudes toward the opposed group, so cursory has been the study. Even more dangerously, a smug attitude is developed that an understanding of the subject is present when in fact the survey has only presented the study's most superficial aspects.

Such attempts at a synoptic approach to learning are at best little more than skin grafting without the attendant follow-up procedures which should normally characterize a clinical operation. We are still violating Whitehead's absolute rule of educational life: "You may not divide the seamless coat of learning." [7]

Since much of the stultification in the meeting of the two cultures arises from a mute insensibility to the language of the opposed group, it is through the development of a sensitivity to both scientific and literary expression at the earliest stages of a child's school life that we would seem to have the greatest chance of success in overcoming our dilemma.

No little acknowledgment has been made in education of the importance of the beginning stages of a child's school life. The question still remains, however: how can we provide concretely the optimum conditions for children's growth in this critical period?

No one today denies that the focal point for provision of the conditions is in the area of learning to read. During the past twenty-five years more attention has been given to the topic of reading instruction than to any other area in the curriculum; extensive research has been undertaken, a multitude of basal readers has been developed, guidebooks have been prepared, and diverse teaching aids have been employed in the tasks.

In all these attempts, the assumption has been made that teachers in the classroom will somehow manage to bring together the varied theories and practices and apply them effectively to the task at hand. This assumption is quite prevalent in teacher-training colleges. Most colleges maintain that their primary responsibility is that of equipping students with skill in the craft of instructing children. The main reason for including such subjects as psychology, sociology, philosophy, and history of education is that these studies provide useful rules for application in the classroom. Although the colleges acknowledge that success in the classroom will depend greatly upon the personal quality of the teacher, this prime datum has received little attention in most teacher-training institutions except through their policies of admission.

Language learning in the early stages of a child's school life has followed, accordingly, a blunderbuss direction of development. Into the program have gone a plethora of methodologies and materials in the hope that by employing disparate shot at least some part of the target would be struck.

It is singularly naïve to continue thinking that all primary teachers can attain a synoptic approach to language teaching in the face of the pressures presently on them. What they do deserve is commendation for the sincerity of their efforts and for the obvious warmth and personal concern which they give to their pupils.

We must assume that the quality of teachers in our

schools will remain constant for many years to come. There will be excellent teachers in our classrooms who will continue to succeed admirably in awakening minds, in spite of all the diversity about them; there will be teachers in our classrooms as well who will do irreparable damage to the minds of children in spite of all the guide-books and materials which are now afforded. What must be done (and here the must is a categorical imperative) is twofold: (1) instruments for learning must be developed to unite science and the humanities whereby the able teachers can do an even more effective job and the medi-ocre or poor teacher can do less damage to growing minds, and (2) the theoretical part of the work of university de-partments of education in the making of teachers must be revised.

It would require much more space than I have here to give an account of what I think needs to be done in the making of teachers. The point I would most want to stress in such an account is that the prime purpose of a teacher's theoretical studies should be to give him the kind of under-standing which makes him a more fully human being than he was before. The educative power of the studies undertaken must come from the student learning to rec-ognize in all great human attainments, be they literary or scientific, the expression of a human nature which he also shares with great men whom he can take as a model for his own achievement. What I am suggesting is that a theory of liberal learning can greatly accelerate a man's progress in the liberal art itself.

I have mentioned the insistent task of making of teachers before discussing instruments for language learning in order to emphasize that ultimately we must aim at improving the quality of language teachers—all teachers for that matter. "Every teacher a teacher of English" has long been the rallying cry in education. A more appropriate slogan would be "Every teacher a teacher of persons and things." Other comments are necessary about the making of teachers, but these comments must now be put into a wider context.

Let there be no illusion—the sort of liberal education we would hope for in the making of teachers can represent at the present time only a distant goal. A feverish pace of more careful selection, more in-service programs, more sabbatical leaves, and more evangelical missions will not accomplish what is needed *now*. The insistent present, however, should not discourage those persons in education departments who are working out a theory of what should be done in teacher education and exemplifying the theory better in practice. William James, in his *Talks to Teachers,* had this to say on imitation:

There is only one way to improve ourselves, and that is by some of us setting an example which the others may pick up and imitate till the new fashion spreads from east to west. Some of us are in more favorable positions than others to set new fashions. Some are much more striking personally and imitable, so to speak. But no living person is sunk so low as not to be imitated by somebody. Thackeray somewhere says of the Irish nation that there never was an Irishman living so poor that he didn't have a still poorer Irishman living at his expense; and, surely, there is no human being whose example doesn't work contagiously in *some* particular. The very idiots at our public institutions imitate each other's peculiarities. And, if you should individually achieve calmness and harmony in your own person, you may depend upon it that a wave of imitation will spread from you, as surely as the circles spread outward when a stone is dropped into a lake.[8]

The message is immediately relevant to the formative work of those education departments which are already setting the pattern for future teacher education.

The effective union of science and the humanities must take place much earlier, however, at a period in people's lives when no separation occurs. To a young child the world of persons and things is full of wonder. As he builds up his own world through spoken language there is astonishment evinced at every turn. This beginning in wonder and culmination in astonishment are the sort of imaginative power which should be prompted into further growth; they are the springboard for studies in both science and poetry.

At this point, I should like to illustrate something of the language powers which children possess before they arrive at school. I take my illustration from diaries written by five-year-old children before they entered into a formal program of instruction. These children possessed a range of intelligence from average to superior. The children did not apparently require a mental age of six years and six months before they undertook the mental feats of reading, writing, and spelling. Given certain conditions for learning, the pupils gained an incredible facility in language as I think these four diaries written spontaneously illustrate.

This morning the fragrant air woke me up. My, it felt as if a cloud were surrounding me. I can't quite express how it felt. Then I went to breakfast.

This morning I got up and saw Laddie looking at me. I thought he was going to bite me so I hid behind the door. Laddie waited a few seconds and came running to the door. He got in and tickled me out.

On Highbury close to Beck, I saw a street sweeper. It is a machine. I watched the rotating brushes. There were five brushes. What a dust!

My grandmother broke her wrist on Valentine Day. Now we think she has the mumps. Yesterday, she had a headache. Boy, what a problem! We sure are in a predicament. Who is going to pay the Dr. Bill? I hope we don't. What a problem!

These illustrations are in part taken out of context because each account is carefully illustrated with a drawing. Here is an indication that the child recognizes the inadequacy of the printed word to express all his ideas about the world of persons and things. In the diaries the children show an amazing perceptiveness in building up their world through language. They also show an awareness of the hopes, joys, and sorrows of persons who are like themselves.

How did these four children manage to accomplish such amazing skill? An investigation of what they had been doing at home indicated that one of the most formative influences was their viewing of television. In contrast to what one might expect, the greatest impact on learning was not the wide range of a so-called "experiential background" received from television. When the children were observed watching television, they were found to be rather passive during the main part of the program, but when the commercial came on the screen, attention was immediately riveted to what was being portrayed.

The advertiser was restricted to a few seconds of program time to accomplish his task of selling. He used as many findings as possible from motivation and marketing research in order to convey his message and sell his product. Stick-figure animation, tachistoscopic presentation of a name or slogan, rhythm, repetition, contrasts, controlled superimposures, and myriad other devices were employed in the effort to sell. Association of symbol and thing was so well established that not only was a product sold but the critical first step in learning to read was accomplished: the children had learned how speech could be represented in writing. This sudden realization—the aha! phenomenon—was enough to prompt an immediate search for more power in written language. The diaries are the result.

I do not for a moment suggest that we should now give our children a solid dose of commercials. The lesson should be quite obvious, however. We must learn from the application of science so that our instructional designs can accomplish what is already a common feature of the market place, but we must do more. The accomplishments of science were not the outcomes of methods left to chance, but of methods which were constantly revised and improved. In my view, we must learn our lessons from science and its applications in such a way that language learning might become accumulative in the same way that scientific endeavors have been accumulative.

The television set itself is a further lesson which we can learn from the applications of science. A simple turning of a knob on the set permits an amazingly complex piece of machinery to be operated with confidence and safety. The innumerable feats of modern technology are the outcomes of intensive studies to determine the ways by which equipment can be operated with maximum ease *and* maximum chance of success. Such a search often means that increased complexity has to be built into the equipment.

The illustration is also closely paralleled in terms of children's oral language development. When the young child, for example, attempts through language to locate persons and things in time, he tests a range of tenses in many contexts. Once he discovers how this locating in language corresponds to the locating of himself and others in time, he builds into his language the new complexity and operates it successfully and confidently.[9] This, by the way, is not handled at any abstract order of theorizing about language, but is handled primarily through the process of comparing.

There is increasing evidence today to suggest that most of the present instructional materials employed to bring about learning to read have failed to take into account this basic principle of ease of operation. Thus, there is still considerable debate as to what should be introduced first: letters, words, phrases, sentences, or the sounds making up the language. These orders of abstraction when presented to the learner can compound the complexities rather than reduce them. Thus vocabulary control in basal readers pays only a cursory attention to the meanings of what is to be read. A welter of perceptual configurations also confronts the child. No encouragement is offered for the learner to discover how words cooperate to handle meanings or to see the correspondence of speech with its written notation. And motivation for learning depends primarily on vicarious enjoyment of stories ostensibly portraying children's interests.

I do not for a moment suggest that we should deny children the opportunities of delight in vicarious experiences, but such forms of motivation for learning to read may be at complete variance with what is known concerning children's basic interests in learning to read. D. O. Hebb, for example, has stated, "The immediate drive value of cognitive processes without intermediary is not only psychologically demonstrable but *has* been demonstrated." [10]

With the commercials on television and with the basal readers, children attempt both consciously and unconsciously to understand the meanings of printed symbols. They implicitly recognize that there is a dimension of language in written form without which they are somehow incomplete. It is unfortunate that the medium of television and of basal readers should hold out the promise of so much good and at the same time lose most of their power through misdirected efforts.

My remarks up to this point may have indicated a considerable degree of pessimism about what has been attempted in bringing about language learning to date. It is appropriate, accordingly, to draw attention to the fact that materials have already been developed for beginning language instruction which do succeed in an amazing number of ways to effect a union of science and the humanities. But here I am simply pointing to prophets who are perhaps not always heard as clearly in their own land as they should be. I refer, of course, to the important work of Professor Richards and his colleague Miss Christine Gibson. [11]

Extensive documentation has been made a number of times of the principles directing their instructional designs. [12] Here, I should simply like to point out some of the ways in which their materials for first steps in reading English embody a collation of the outcomes of many scientific studies.

There is in the material an acknowledgment made of the fact that by the time a child comes to school he is in a very real sense a consummate grammarian. In the Richards-Gibson material the child is invited to learn how words cooperate to handle meanings which are immediately picturable. The language used in the initial sentences touches off those language powers which a child already possesses and encourages the learner into further growth in language.

From a neurological point of view such a procedure is sound. There is, within the brain, an area called by the neurologist the reticular formation, which serves to stimulate and excite the organism into activity. Too much stimulation results in a random, unordered type of behavior that increasingly engenders tension. Faced with mounting pressures, the learner adopts a wide variety of strategies in order to reduce the tension. Any careful study of how children are conceiving the meanings of printed symbols with present day materials indicates the diversity of strategies that are employed. This trial and error form of learning may succeed in a partial way in terms of scores on achievement tests, but viewed within a continuum of learning, the faulty strategies established at the early stages can remain to plague the learner in his later development. In contrast, the Richards-Gibson material aims at helping the learner to enter directly into the task of finding out successfully how language works.

The design of the sequences is closely paralleled in much

of the work being done on programmed learning. Thus, each step confirms what has gone before and prepares for what is to follow. There is a minimal time delay between a learner taking a step and finding out whether the step has been taken successfully. The systematic reduction of perceptual problems is directly related to current thinking about the importance of reducing error possibilities. "Nothing succeeds like success" is an observation now well substantiated by experimental evidence, but success in this instance is the increasing feeling of mastery over a task at hand. The material prepared by Richards and Gibson aims at touching off something of the deepest in mankind's motivation: that work in itself can be its own reward whatever other extraneous rewards might accrue.

Experimental evidence on what children do in learning while working with such material is still rather sparse. Enough has been done, however, to point out some encouraging signs. Thus, the writing and spelling of language is an implicit outgrowth from the work that is done in learning to read. Further, the learners evince a spontaneity in handling words in their speech and their writing with a proficiency quite different from that of pupils fed on a richer, unordered diet. When learners develop for themselves a language instrument which is not a load on the memory, increased opportunities are provided for them to mount imaginative conceptions about persons or things. They can do this more effectively not only in speech and writing but also in their general ordering of perceptions. Thus pupils who have worked with the Richards-Gibson material have been found to exhibit an increased awareness of persons and things even to the place where they include this awareness in their drawings.[13]

All this is not to suggest that with such material a teacher need do nothing more in bringing about the learning of English. What it does do, however, is to make more effective the work of the discerning teacher and obviates many of the dangers inherent in the type of teaching which is simply an affair of rules without any reference to later learning.

The other aspect of the material requires attention here. Working with the material as a group engaged in a common task, children evince some amazing forms of social growth. And here I do not refer just to an increase in social adjustment on the part of the children. An intellectual and emotional development has been found to occur in somewhat the same order as the description made of education by William Cory over one hundred years ago:

You go to a great school not for knowledge so much as for arts and habits; for the habit of attention, for the art of expression, for the art of assuming at a moment's notice a new intellectual posture, for the art of entering quickly into another person's thought, for the habit of submitting to censure and refutation, for the art of indicating assent or dissent in graduated terms, for the habit of regarding minute points of accuracy, for the habit of working out what is possible in a given time, for taste, for discrimination, for mental courage and mental soberness. Above all, you go to a great school for self-knowledge.[14]

It has been found that children five years of age can learn how to attend when tackling difficult tasks, how to profit from someone else's successes and failures, and how to aid others in their learning. They can learn, as well, how to enter quickly into another person's thought and feeling and can learn to examine their own intellectual efforts at every turn. Such social growth was found to be directly related to the sort of invitation to learn set before them.[15]

Enough is known already about the procedures to warrant extensive exploration on a much wider scale. Given a sound foundation in language, it is quite conceivable that both science and the humanities can come into their own in a synoptic way based on the same principles of simplification theory implicit in the early reading materials suggested. But for this part of the task we shall require a different sort of study than has been at all common in educational research. We can no longer be content with the sort of "controlled experiment" that ostensibly compares the merits of one procedure as contrasted with another. Cronbach has stated that there is a limited usefulness of sheerly empirical generalizations no matter how huge the samples on which they are based. He suggests that research should put greater emphasis on instensive studies perhaps with small samples which "will yield understanding about changes in behaviour rather than isolated facts about scores." [16] We must be concerned, in effect, just as much with the mental processes whereby scores are obtained as with the scores.

The early beginnings of language power demand an extensive revision in all the invitations which are set before children in their learning. It is not enough simply to provide a stage upon which abstractions such as set-theory principles, problem solving, conservation of matter, historical causation, and the rest can be placed. There are ample indications today that we are on the frontier of a reordering of curriculum in our public and secondary schools. Bruner has set the picture in perspective with his report on the Woods Hole Conference.[17] Even more concretely we have the very practical outcomes of such groups as the School Mathematics Group, the University of Illinois Mathematics Project, The Physical Science Study Committee and, in Canada, a comparable beginning has been made by such organizations as the Mathematics Commission and the Toronto Board of Education-University Committee. These meetings of minds of persons working at various levels of education suggest that significant outcomes may accrue in our attainment of synoptic views of *all* studies.

But a word of caution is appropriate here; all this committee work and the phenomenal development of programmed learning could easily lead to the place where we shall succeed in doing more effectively something which should never have been done in the first place. I suggest that university education departments have a critical responsibility in the next few years to see that these spontaneous outbursts of enthusiasm will take some unified form. I suggest, in turn, that the development of a synoptic approach to language learning could be the medium through which concrete form could be given to the union of science and the humanities. It is vitally important to see that the instructional designs employed to bring about learning of any study does embody an increasing order of language development.

For example, the simplification employed to bring about the learning of a mathematical principle through programmed instruction demands that the programmer must have an immediate awareness of the ordering of language. Most programs today fail on just that point. But even beyond this, countless opportunities are provided whereby the learner can discover new insights into language—and new proficiencies—while his immediate concern might seem to be mathematics. Again, let me repeat that separation of mental activity into subjects is nonexistent in a child's mind.

The tasks are rather formidable but can be accomplished, I suggest, through a clear recognition of the contributions which can be made by persons of various disciplines meeting together with the primary purpose of improving concrete practice. To facilitate the meeting we are going to require an administrative organization which might be called an institute of instructional design. Such an organization would include expert teachers from elementary and secondary schools and universities. It would also include persons who have made such an intensive study of a particular subject that they have become in a real sense philosophical in their outlook.

On this point I should remind you that many of the significant ideas which we hold as wisdom in education have come from persons who were first of all not concerned with the tasks of teaching. Their understanding is of the order of the meaning of "understand" in the French proverb "To understand all is to forgive all." These are the sorts of persons we need to give form and substance to the principles which we would most want our pupils to appreciate in the early stages of learning. It is the responsibility of those persons who have an understanding of a subject to make the principles of the discipline manageable *through language* in the minds of young boys and girls.

I suggest that another group of persons is required in such an institute. These are the persons who are questioning continuously some of the basic assumptions which the other persons might be making about the nature of childhood. I refer to those persons who have studied what children are like in school not on a purely descriptive level but with the sort of philosophical thinking embodied in much of Piaget's work.

It will be seen that this type of organization is charged with the responsibility of keeping in balance a program of instructional design which might take the diagrammatic form of an equilateral triangle, where the base represents the nature of the study, one side represents agreement on what principles of the study should be learned, and the remaining side the possibilities for learning exhibited by children. But such balance will only accrue when there is a clear recognition on the part of all persons that it is through increasing language power that we can enter most effectively into the thought and feeling of either the poet or the scientist.

There is no doubt in my mind that such an organization in education departments would go far to re-establish in the academic world a prestige which has somehow fallen into considerable disrepute. Further, it would emphasize the responsibilities of *all* departments in the development of young persons. For in spite of what Robert Frost says, good fences do not make good neighbors in education.

I envisage that institutes of instructional design would be immediately concerned with new media such as teaching machines, films, textbooks, television, radio, language laboratories, and so on. The sort of critical inquiry which would ensue could place an educational dimension on these media which is lacking at the moment and obviate the serious dangers of too much commercialism.

My comments may seem far removed from the topic of language learning. To try to suggest now the sort of re-ordering which is necessary in language learning curricula, the types of textbooks we most need, or the activities that should characterize classroom practice would be to defeat the main thesis which I have been attempting to advance.

I do know that what passes for a curriculum in English and second languages at the elementary-school level is in just as much need of re-examination as mathematics or science. But I do not suggest that such reordering must come about in isolation from the study of the sciences or social sciences.

When institutes of instructional design come to examine curricula in English and second-language learning, I predict that many of our ideas about the studies will be changed. Simplification of first steps in reading—of the sort I have suggested—must mean that our concept of readiness will be changed since readiness automatically begs the question: readiness for what? Simplification of instructional design in other studies and the union of science and the humanities must mean that much of the abstract theorizing about language which now occupies a considerable portion of the elementary-school curriculum can be deferred to a later period, when abstract theorizing can be of better value. Thus the study of how words cooperate in problem solving in mathematics is more relevant to the young child than any general theorizing about language which we might give him through a study of conventional grammar. The setting for studies of language-learning curricula will have to center on the questions of what should come before what, when, and in what order. The articulated program proposed as a hypothesis by the Modern Language Association needs testing, but, I suggest, it must be done within the synoptic framework that is now emerging.

When new media have been assigned a sound educational dimension, it is quite possible that the time for learning will be shortened; already there are indications that this will be so from the initial trials of programmed instruction. Given this time and the increased understanding engendered by well-designed instructional materials, the teacher can enter a role which she should always have had. Thus encouraging imaginative powers, pointing up implications of what has been learned, and assisting pupils who are having difficulties could become a strong feature of her work in place of her present role as a purveyor of snippets of knowledge, an evaluator of exercise books, and a rushed clinician in handling pupils' difficulties.

I endorse no pessimistic view that such events are impossible. There are enough signs discernible today that significant progress has already been made in the direction I have attempted to point out. The insistence of the tasks demands that we must accelerate our pace.

THE INGLIS LECTURE

The Developing Imagination

NORTHROP FRYE

THE INGLIS LECTURESHIP

To honor the memory of Alexander Inglis, 1879–1924, his friends and colleagues gave to the Graduate School of Education, Harvard University, a fund for the maintenance of a Lectureship in Secondary Education. It is the purpose of the Lectureship to perpetuate the spirit of the labors of Professor Inglis in secondary education and contribute to the solution of problems in this field.

The Developing Imagination

NORTHROP FRYE

I am not, like my friend Mr. MacKinnon, an expert in the field with which my lecture is concerned. My own preparatory education I regarded, rightly or wrongly, as one of the milder forms of penal servitude, and it was fortunate for me that in my easygoing days I could enter school at grade four and the University of Toronto from grade eleven. So I probably owe my present interest in education to the fact that I had so little of it. However, I have acquired the seniority which is the natural reward of survival, and I now find myself sitting on committees concerned with every stage of the education continuum from kindergarten to graduate school.* I still do not know very much about what is taught in Ontario high schools, especially in the upper grades which I never reached, but I do know something of what is said at

* This paper is closely related to my introduction to the reports of the study committees appointed by the Joint Committee of the Board of Education of Toronto and the University of Toronto (*Design for Learning,* University of Toronto Press, 1962).

Ontario high school commencements, as I have said a fair amount of it myself. I propose therefore to take the commencement perspective rather than the classroom perspective, and to confine myself to the only area of learning in which I can claim any scholarly competence, which is that of English language and literature.

I teach literature at the upper university levels, and in recent years have given most of my attention to the theory of criticism. In the old humanist days, when literary training was confined to the classical languages, contact with one's own literature was left largely to what was called "taste," a by-product rather than a definite subject of education. When modern literatures became a subject of academic study, toward the latter half of the nineteenth century, the philological scholarship developed in the classics was naturally first applied to them. Since then, scholarship in modern literature has become a flourishing enough discipline, but we have not yet evolved a literary criticism which is solidly based on this scholarship, which clarifies its central principles, brings its assumptions into the open, and provides a view of the whole subject giving proportion and context to its more restricted achievements.

We have not even evolved a theory of criticism which can distinguish the genuine from the useless in scholarship itself. This distinction is left to the common sense of the scholar, which is usually but by no means invariably the best place to leave it. We still encounter students who have been awarded Ph.D.'s for theses on made-up subjects that are of no use to anyone, least of all the student. We can say that the supervisor of such a thesis has been a fathead, but in the absence of critical theory we cannot speak of academic malpractice. There is a bewildering amount of scholarship and commentary and piecemeal criticism today—far too much for anyone to keep up with more than odd bits of it—but very little understanding of the central principles of the study of literature. Our critical theory, as reflected in our teaching at all levels, is still largely the old "taste," or "appreciation," reinforced by a variety of "backgrounds," biographical, historical, and linguistic, none of which seem to contribute directly or systematically to the problem described in Wordsworth's *Prelude* as the impairing and restoring of taste.

Although most literary scholarship, good or bad, is intelligible only to fairly advanced university students, it is natural that its unpruned vine, a wild tangle of foliage with few identifying flowers or fruits, should be creeping around the schools as well, in the form of explicatory and other teaching methods. But the issues involved are more important than that. In the first place, the only guarantee that a subject is theoretically coherent is its ability to have its elementary principles taught to children. In the second place, literature cannot be directly taught or learned: what is taught and learned is the criticism of literature, and whatever is hard to understand about the place of literature in education owes its difficulty to the confusion of critical theory. I sympathize entirely with the plea for a more synoptic view of the different subjects taught to children, but how can literature (that is, criticism) enter into such a synoptic view until it has acquired a synoptic view of itself? We are asked to define a pachyderm when we are still collecting blind men's impressions of an elephant.

The subject generally referred to, in English-speaking countries, as "English" means two things. It is the name of a literature which is part of one of the major arts, and it is the mother tongue, the normal means of understanding anything that is not mathematical. Mr. MacKinnon has dealt mainly with the latter aspect; my own chief interest is in the former. I am aware of the dangers of trying to split the mind up into separate faculties, but the different directions that the mind faces, so to speak, surely do need to be distinguished. The faculty addressed by English as a literature is the imagination. At least, that is what the great Romantic critics called it, and I am not aware that the conception has been altered except for the worse. The faculty addressed by English as the mother tongue is one that is often associated, sometimes correctly, with the reason. I should prefer to call it something more like "sense." It is the power of apprehending what is presented to us by experience, the recognition of things as they are. It is the reality principle that we appeal to as the standard of the "normal" in behavior, and it is the basis of the scientific attitude to nature or the external world. The arts, including literature, are not so much concerned with the world as it is: their concern is with the world that man is trying to build out of nature, and the

34

imagination they appeal to is a constructive power, which is neither reason nor emotion, though including elements of both.

It seems to me that there are a primary and a secondary phase of learning which correspond roughly, though by no means exactly, with the chronological stages of our elementary and secondary schools. There is also a tertiary phase, which has a much less direct parallel with post-secondary education, especially in the university. In each phase there is a conservative and a radical aspect of learning, a power of consolidating and a power of exploration and advance. In the primary phase the consolidating or conservative power is memory, and the exploring or radical power is what we have just called "sense." The memory preserves the facts transmitted in text or notebook; but facts, when really understood, are illustrations of principles, and the principles are what the "sense" attempts to grasp. The dull teacher, and the dull student, depend as much on memory and use as little "sense" as possible; and even the good student will rely on his memory to help him through the subjects in which he is less interested. What the memory holds we call content; what sense holds is structure. The good teacher is distinguished from his mediocre colleagues mainly by the efforts he makes to transform content into structure, to help his students to see significant patterns in facts, and to encourage the child to ask "Why?" with more purpose and direction than he ordinarily employs with that word.

Mathematics and the physical sciences are the most theoretically coherent of all the subjects of education, and we can see the supremacy of structure to content most clearly in them. They also best illustrate the fact that the natural shape of elementary teaching is deductive. Elementary science consists of principles so well established that no experiment could do more than simply illustrate them, and almost anything the child encounters in ordinary experience, such as the fact that he gets warmer when he runs, may be used as an illustration of a scientific principle. The teaching of elementary science can be considerably simplified once its deductive shape is realized, and it can also be brought down to the capacities of the youngest learners. (Of course saying that elementary science is presented deductively is not saying that experiment and direct observation are unimportant, at any stage. I knew of one school principal who held that children should not attempt experiments, on the ground that they worked out better when adults did them; hence his students were compelled to stand helplessly by while their rivals in the next precinct were rigging up various gadgets including a burglar alarm, which, after several teachers had walked into it, finally caught a burglar.)

In history, and in at least political geography, the deductive pattern is more difficult to bring out. In Spenser's allegory of the House of Alma, in *The Faerie Queene*, history is entrusted to an old man in the back of the brain called "good memory" (Eumnestes), and it is hardly possible to avoid committing to memory a large number of

36

dates and facts and names before much of a significant pattern can be glimpsed behind them. History, as Burke pointed out long ago, is, along with politics, naturally empirical and inductive in shape, and the difficulty in fitting it into elementary education is greater in consequence. The process may be easier when society is committed to an a priori and deductive view of history, as the Soviet Union is. Complaints that citizens of the democracies, in comparison with Communists, do not know what they really believe in, reflect what may be ultimately a problem of elementary education.

The teaching of literature in school will clearly depend for its tactics on whether literature (or criticism, as above) is naturally deductive in shape, like the physical sciences and mathematics, or naturally inductive, like history. The work I have done on critical theory has convinced me that literature is, like mathematics, mainly structure rather than content, and that the teaching of it, or criticism, can follow a deductive pattern. If I am right, the role of literature in the educational process should become much clearer, and its teaching greatly simplified.

In childhood the imagination is a third force, playing a role subordinate to memory and sense in the schoolroom, if not in the child's mind. In the child's mind it is extremely active, but it is not yet a constructive power: it is still on the level of what Coleridge and other critics distinguish as fancy, a stylizing and modifying of the actual conditions of the child's life, a kind of primitive realism. We can see

37

this fanciful quality in children's pictures and poems, though our critical concepts are usually too vague to separate it from anything else in the "creative" area. The word "creative" is one of the most elastic and elusive metaphors in the language, as befits its theological origin. In any case it is memory and sense that take the lead in learning the techniques of reading and writing.

Those who never get beyond the primary phase of learning illustrate the child's situation in a petrified adult form. They often assume that good memory is equivalent to high intelligence, and (at least recently) that high intelligence is dramatized in the kind of television program in which the possessor of a great deal of noncontroversial information is rewarded with encyclopedias. They also regard literature and the arts as not strictly educational, but as either "frills" on education or as fanciful, concerned with the relaxing or amusing of the mind. In their conception of society, the creative man follows the practical one at a respectful distance. They also tend to make associative judgments, attaching the content of picture or poem to their experience instead of grasping the formal unity of the work. The suggestion that the arts are radically constructive, that they cannot always be directly related to the recognition of reality, but create their own kind of reality, is one that they normally resist or resent.

I referred above to the humanist tradition in education, a form of education based primarily on literature. The strength of humanism lay in its exploitation of a central fact about literature: that the arts do not, like the sciences, evolve and improve, but revolve around classics or models. Like most such principles, this one could be and often was frozen into a sacrosanct dogma, and those who held it in this form give us a sharp sense of its limitations. The Elizabethan Roger Ascham wrote *The Scholemaster* to explain how Latin could be taught by using Cicero as a model. Toward the end of his book he considers, reluctantly, the question whether Cicero really is an example of what he calls "the vnspotted proprietie of the Latin tong . . . at the hiest pitch of all perfitenesse." He is not slow to give his answer:

> For he, that can neither like *Aristotle* in Logicke and Philosophie, nor *Tullie* in Rhetoricke and Eloquence, will from these steppes, likelie enough presume, by like pride, to mount hier, to the misliking of greater matters: that is either in Religion, to haue a dissentious head, or in the common wealth, to haue a factious hart: as I knew one a student in Cambridge, who, for a singularitie, began first to dissent, in the scholes, from *Aristotle,* and sone after became a peruerse *Arian,* against Christ and all true Religion.

Nevertheless, the humanist theory of models worked fairly well in literary education, because it is broadly true for literature, and in addition it had the great advantage of being deductive in shape, giving the student a few central texts and extracting from them a set of principles he could apply in all his reading, and more particularly in all his writing. But, of course, the humanist theory was inadequate for the inductive sciences, where classical authority has no functional place.

Humanistic education was directed toward the past: the essential standards and values already existed in certain classics, and they could be applied to present use. Its curriculum, as the quotation from Ascham indicates, could be taught with the greatest confidence in both the subject matter and the ethical validity of its classics. There they were, dignified and eminently visible. Education slowly began to change its center of gravity from literature to science about a century ago, and this meant a change to an education directed not toward the past but toward a present and an unknown future, where anything we now know may be rendered obsolete by coming discoveries. Hence the social and moral values established by education have tended to become interim values. Many educators have naturally attempted to transfer the public confidence in education from the past to the present and future, from establishment to process, to new programs of what has been alternately called education for today and education for tomorrow. But an uncertainty about the content and the purpose of education, a sense of lost values, and an uneasiness about the loss are plain for anyone to see. I am not proposing any "return" to humanism as a cure for this; still, the question naturally suggests itself: is there anything permanent in humanism, and appropriate at least to the literary part of education today, that can be re-established within its present context?

We notice that literature is, by its very nature, intensely allusive: its classics or models, once recognized as such, echo and re-echo through all subsequent ages. Whitman urged us to make less of the wrath of Achilles and develop new themes for a new world, where the Muse would be invoked to sing of the righteous wrath of an American democrat. But allusions to Homer in writers even more recent than Whitman carry the same weight of authority that they carried in Milton's day, and Whitman's view clearly does not fit the facts of literary experience. It looks as though that experience were not a random one, but radiated from a center where the great classics, including Homer, are to be found. Literature revolves around certain classics or models because it is really revolving around certain structural principles which those classics embody. The problem of imitation or mimesis in literature has two aspects. The traditional imitation of nature (or action, or life, or experience) refers primarily to content, but as far as his form is concerned, what the poet imitates are the conventions and genres of literature as he finds them. This latter aspect of literature is so neglected in our teaching of it that we tend to make naïve judgments on literature which assume that literary works form a kind of continuous allegorical commentary on the society contemporary with them. Thus if a dramatist writes a play without succeeding in giving it any dramatic shape, he can always say that its shapelessness reflects the chaos of our time. It does nothing of the kind, of course: what it reflects is probably the practice of a better dramatist who gives a skillful illusion of shapelessness, and that practice in its turn reflects, not the chaos of our time, but a stage in the development of certain twentieth-century dramatic conventions.

The humanist theory, in its earliest stages, based the study of literature on precept and example. It was the *sententiae,* the profound axioms of the human situation, that were especially prized in the great writers, and the stories they told were *exempla,* or illustrations of the same kind of thing. This approach puts literature at the service of certain social and moral ideals assumed to be permanently valid. No doubt it is an important function of literature, especially in childhood, to reinforce with its peculiar resonance the kind of attitudes we want our children to accept. I have been fascinated by Mr. MacKinnon's account of the effectiveness of television commercials as teaching techniques, which are also based on *sententiae,* in the form of advertising slogans, and pretend to have the same kind of moral urgency. Apparently Marxism, in its later or post-Lenin phase, holds much the same conception of the social role of literature. Granting that there are better forms of such an approach, they would still be primarily rhetorical, training the student in English as the mother tongue, and only incidentally in English as part of a major art. We need along with this a genuinely literary conception of English, based on structure rather than content, on insight rather than memory, one which will give literarture its own proper independence instead of making it an adjunct of accepted modes of life and manners.

One essential aspect of literary training, and one that it is possible to acquire, or begin acquiring, in childhood, is the art of listening to stories. This sounds like a passive ability, but it is not passive at all: it is what the army would call a basic training for the imagination. It is the opposite of the sententious approach, because the mind is directed toward total structure, not to piecemeal content. Concentrating on a story separates the work of the reason, which proceeds by argument and thesis, by aggression and dialectical conflict, from the proper work of the imagination, where there are no assertions and no refutations. The storyteller asserts nothing: he lays down postulates. The postulates may be, for example, that a little girl goes to sleep outdoors one afternoon, sees a rabbit run past her, sees him take a watch out of his pocket and mutter something about being late for an appointment, and follows him as he disappears down a rabbit-hole. Very well: these are the storyteller's postulates; we listen to the story to see what he does with them. We learn to suspend judgment until more data are in—a useful habit of mind in itself. We learn not to argue or raise objections before our perspective is in focus, and when all objections are still only prejudices. (The appropriate Socratic dialogue would run somewhat as follows: "But that's silly; rabbits don't talk or look at watches." "Well, they do in this story: now shut up.") If in later years we are confronted with nonobjective painting, twelve-tone music, or the theater of the absurd, our early training should help us to try to grasp first of all the totality of what is presented. Failing such training, we are apt to try to assimilate the work of art to the discursive and argumentative structures of words that we are more familiar with, and ask such questions as: What is he trying to get across? Why can't somebody explain it to me? and the like.

The next question is what stories it is particularly appropriate for a child to listen to, and here we come back again to the fact that literature is allusive, and seems to radiate from a center. Literature develops out of, or is preceded by, a body of myths, legends, folk tales, which are transmitted by our earlier classics. In our tradition the most important groups of these myths are the biblical and the classical, and it is essential to acquire some knowledge of both as early in life as possible. One reason for doing so is sheer convenience: these stories are so endlessly alluded to and commented on that one has no landmarks in literature without them. To grow up in ignorance of what is in the Bible or Homer is as crippling to the imagination as being deprived of the multiplication table. But convenience in understanding allusions is not the really important reason for knowing the sources of them.

The really important reason, as far as literature is concerned, is that there are only a certain number of ways (structural principles) in which stories can be told, and

44

familiarity with two major mythologies, the Greek and the biblical, puts us in command of all of them. In other words, there really is a deductive principle in literature which can be exploited for educational purposes. All stories in literature are developments of fundamental fictional shapes which can be studied most clearly in myths and folk tales. The reason why writers are so persistently fascinated by myth and folk tale is not antiquarianism, but the fact that, like still life in painting, they illustrate the formal characteristics of their art most clearly. Some students of mine now in secondary schools tell me that they have had a good deal of success in teaching the writing of fiction by using the principle that I call "displacement," giving their students a myth or a Grimm fairy tale and asking them to translate each detail of it into a plausible or realistic incident, while preserving the structure intact.

From familiarity with the traditional stories of our culture we may gradually acquire a sense of the categories of stories, which I should classify as four in number: the romantic, the comic, the tragic, and the ironic. Of these, comedy and romance are primary; tragedy and irony more difficult, because more ambivalent in tone. Once again, those who never get past the primary phase of learning seldom read anything with genuine pleasure that is not a comedy or a romance. The next step is to get a sense of structure as exhibited in the conventions and genres of literature. We notice that when we read deliberately for relaxation, we turn to highly conventionalized stories where the general structure is known in advance, such as the detective story, the Western, or the even more predictable dramas of television.

The distinction between the structure and the texture of fiction, which criticism has only begun to recognize, is of major importance in determining the sequence of reading. The really difficult writers who have to be reserved for the university, such as Proust or Conrad or the later Henry James, are as a rule more difficult in texture, but keep to much the same principles of structure as the writers we are more inclined to take to bed with us. Complex writers attract a great deal of rather myopic commentary, based entirely on texture, which with a better training in structure might be less necessary for students to read, or, if they become advanced students, to write. Works of universal appeal and of great and immediate communicative power are usually simple in texture as well as structure. Hence they, or something in them, are primary in the educational sequence.

The traditional humanists identified such works with the classics of Greek and Latin literatures: this identification is still going strong in Matthew Arnold's essay "The Choice of Subjects in Poetry." We need a broader principle of the same type, such as the real principle that underlies Tolstoy's *What is Art?*

In its present form Tolstoy's theory is a tissue of exclusive value judgments based on nonliterary values—in other words it is critically neurotic. But it would make a good deal of sense if transformed into an educational theory, used to establish the central texts that could be used with profit by children and others of limited imaginative experience. We have all met or heard of people of little formal schooling, who know the Bible and a few English classics and give the impression of essentially educated people. I suggest that the impression is based, not on sentimental illusion, but on the facts of literary education. And it is still possible to say that one who does not know the central classics of his own language and cultural tradition gives the impression of an ignoramus, regardless of what else he knows.

In the secondary phase of education, the radical and conservative aspects of learning become more conceptual. They are now closer to the radicalism and conservatism distinguished by John Stuart Mill in the political thought of his day, and in fact they are most easily seen at work in the social and political area. In the secondary phase the radical side of the mind wants to know what good or what use an idea or institution is, whether we could get along without it, what it has to say for itself even if generally accepted. The conservative side wants to know why the idea or institution exists, why it has been accepted if wrong, what significance is in the fact that it has existed. Thus the secondary phase revolves around the problem of symbolism, of the relation of appearance to reality, and its aim is not simply the formation of an intelligence, as in the primary phase, but the formation of a critical intelligence, the intelligence of a responsible citizen in a complex modern democracy.

In this phase the growing imaginative power forms a natural alliance with the conservative side of learning. The radical side is utilitarian, aggressive, argumentative, appealing to what it regards as reason or common sense, and it is frequently anti-imaginative. It is impressed by the actuality of the present, as the conservative side is by the inadequacy of the present to what one's deeper desires demand. The imagination is no longer fanciful, and it is not yet a fully constructive power, but moves most freely among the monuments of its own magnificence. It is bound intellectually to tradition, and emotionally to nostalgia. The problem in our society recently tagged with the phrase "two cultures" refers to a natural division in the mental attitudes of most of our educated citizens. It is considerably oversimplifying the problem to identify the two attitudes with the sciences and the humanities respectively.

In stressing the importance of myth and of biblical and classical stories in primary literary education, I am agreeing to some extent with the outline of an "articulated English program" recently proposed by a committee of the Modern Language Association. Mr. MacKinnon refers to this in passing, but without much enthusiasm, and it is clear that it does not, for him, solve the problem of relating literary to other aspects of education. My own feeling is, once again, that whatever separates literature from the rest of education reflects the confusion of critical theory. As long as a story is just a story, the real separation involved is the separation of fiction from fact—in itself, of course, a healthy and necessary separation. But some stories are more obviously just stories than others. The radical side of our critical intelligence may assert that the story of the Garden of Eden in Genesis is on precisely the same plane of reality as the Garden of the Hesperides in Homer. But the conservative side, aided by the imagination, realizes that the myth of creation and fall in Genesis has been and still is an informing principle of our religious, social, and even philosophical thought, whether we are conscious of its role in those areas or not.

The extent to which our thinking is molded by informing principles articulated in poetic myths is still largely an unexplored subject in literary criticism. It is most highly developed, I think, in the criticism of American literature, but the books that set it forth are difficult books, addressed to advanced scholars, and have not made much headway into the educational system. Still, most serious students of American literature are aware that *Huckleberry Finn, Moby Dick, The Scarlet Letter, Walden,* the tales of Poe, and others can be studied not only as works of literature but as focal points of a cultural imagination, and that as such they make American history, politics, religion, and social life more intelligible. Literary works which express these informing social myths most clearly are the works which have prior claim on the educator's attention, whenever they can be read or adapted for reading. They are not invariably the books of greatest literary value, though they always have some value: they would include, for instance, *Uncle Tom's Cabin*.

It is of course true that a great deal of trash which passes as literature, or at least as entertaining reading, also articulates social myths with great clarity. I read many of the novels of Horatio Alger at an early age, and as I have a good verbal memory, a journey round my skull would unearth a great many pages of some of the most pedestrian prose on record. I wish very much that a surgical operation could remove it and substitute something better, but still Alger probably did me no permanent damage, as I was never inspired to adopt the virtues of his heroes, and this leads me to hope that the children of today may emerge similarly unscathed from their similar experiences. I feel that a well-planned literary education would give us a standard by which to measure such writing. By a standard I do not mean only a standard of quality or value, which any literary education worth anything at all would give: I mean also a standard of comprehension, an understanding of it not merely as bad writing but as shoddy mythology. The benefits of having such a standard of comprehension extend far beyond literature. I should think, for example, that the doctrines of Mr. Buckley or Senator Goldwater would have little appeal to a society in which the high school graduates knew something about the working of pastoral myth in the political imagination.

I am well aware that what I suggest bears a close resemblance to one of the worst and most futile ways of teaching literature. This is the practice of reducing every work of imagination to a sociological document, studying Henry James or Faulkner merely as illustrating some dismal clichés about cultural decline in New England or the Old South. The emphasis I should prefer is the exact reverse of this. Historians and social scientists give most of their conscious attention to inductive procedures, the collecting of facts and evidence. They give much less attention to the conceptions that give shape and organization to the books they write, conceptions which are therefore largely unconscious, but are revealed in such things as the choice of metaphors and analogies. These conceptions are really myths, using the word "myth" in its proper sense of an informing verbal structure, and literature enables us to understand what these myths are. As I have maintained elsewhere, literature has an informing relation to the verbal disciplines somewhat analogous to the relation of mathematics to the physical sciences.

The same principles would apply to the study of English as a foreign or a second language. Looking at English or American culture from the outside gives one a different perspective on it, certainly. French poets found not only an American but a universal cultural significance in Poe that we have been slow to discover for ourselves, and Lenin's view of Jack London has given him an importance in Russia that he has never had in his own country. But while the perspectives are different, they are not irreconcilably different. We are committed to our own society, but education ought to give us more detachment, to impress us with the importance of satire and denunciation and protest in a healthy culture. A study of the same culture that begins in detachment or even hostility would naturally tend, in itself, to greater sympathy or even a sense of participation. We all know, vaguely, that *Robinson Crusoe* is one of our educational "classics," but a citizen of Asia or Africa might spot more quickly than we the cultural myth that helps to make it a classic. Crusoe lands on his island and instantly opens a journal and a ledger, though all he has to put in the latter are the pros and cons of his situation. He domesticates some animals and ensures himself some privacy—he has no need for privacy, but an Englishman's home is his castle. He catches his man Friday and proceeds to convert him, without the slightest sense of incongruity, to his own brand of modified Presbyterianism. He is the British Empire in action, imposing its own pattern wherever it is, and never dreaming of "going native." The African or Asian is familiar with the social results of Western expansion: if he reads *Robinson Crusoe* he is seeing the same process from the inside, as a conceivable way of life. He may not like its effects any better, but he can see its causes as human and not demonic, and I doubt if education can do much more than that for the brotherhood of man.

These two cultural impulses, a growing detachment from what we possess and a growing sympathy with what is alien, are equally essential in a world like ours. It is reassuring to find a naïve enthusiasm for yoga or Zen Buddhism in the United States: it would be disturbing to find it in India or Japan. The members of the Athenian assemblies who authorized the expedition to Syracuse and the massacre of Mytilene did not know that their culture would come to symbolize sweetness and light, the triumph of reason and beauty over the arid fanaticism of the moral will. But such is the healing power of what is called aesthetic distance. I think that if Hellenism can come to symbolize a love of beauty, and Hebraism a moral energy, the cultural heritage of the English-speaking nations can also come to symbolize a sense of individual freedom which is one of the permanent achievements of human history, and will remain so however dark and troubled our future may become. But it is not for us to dwell on this: our sustained admiration must be rather for other cultures, with hope that we may give some cause, at least to posterity, for admiration of our own.

There are many other aspects of literary education than those of myth and fiction which I have no space to develop. We are greatly confused at present by the notion that prose is the language of ordinary speech, and that poetry is an unnatural and perversely ingenious method of distorting prose statements. We can get a better progression if we realize that the language of ordinary speech is no more prose than it is poetry. The language of ordinary speech is an unshaped associative babble, a series of asyntatic short phrases, and it is psychologically a monologue, designed for expression and not primarily for communication. As it develops toward communication, it can be conventionalized in either of two ways. The direct and simple way is to put a pattern of recurrence on it and turn it into verse. The more difficult and sophisticated way is to put a logical pattern on it and turn it into prose. Developed techniques of verse usually precede developed techniques of prose in the history of literature, because verse is the more primitive of the two. If we listen to small children, we soon realize that their chanting speech has at least as much verse in it as prose. If we mark the essays of college freshmen, we soon realize that we are usually not reading prose, but a series of phrases for which the only appropriate form of punctuation is the dash. The conviction that written language is normally prose, that its unit is the sentence, and that a period goes at the end of it is one that twelve years of concentrated teaching often fails to evoke. The simplest form of literary expression, and the one most readily accessible to children, is, I should think, accentual verse, of the kind that we find in nursery rhymes, and which illustrates the affinity of poetry with dance and song and bodily energy. A lucid prose style accompanies the sense of the complete reality of other people, and its development is a long-range one.

It is partly because of the rhythm of speech in childhood,

54

and partly because of the central role of memory in elementary learning, that sequential and rhythmical catalogues, from the multiplication table to the monarchs of England, are easier for children than for most adults. In this respect children resemble the poets of primitive societies, who are culturally in a parallel situation, unlocking their word hoards to chant their memorized songs of ancestral legends, place names, neighboring tribes and alliterating kings.

In simpler societies this power of memory is the basis of a poetic power of an extraordinarily spontaneous and plastic kind. We find it in ballads and folktales, where motifs and refrains are constantly interchanging and developing new variants. We find it in the formulaic oral epic, with its basis of stock themes and metrical units, described in Professor Lord's fascinating book, *The Singer of Tales* (Cambridge, Mass., 1960). We can find it in other arts, as in some schools of Oriental painting, which develop out of what are essentially memorized subjects. Many of the strongest cultural movements of our time seem to be headed in a somewhat similar direction: in action painting, in the genuine forms of jazz music, in certain poetic developments often and not too accurately associated with the term "beat." Professor Lord has shown for the formulaic epic that spontaneity shrivels instantly at the touch of education, or at any rate of book learning, and some of the contemporary phenomena just listed seem to have a strongly anti-intellectual slant to them. Yet the analogies between the primitive and the childlike may need further exploration in an age where there are so many media of education that circumvent the normal book learning processes and cut straight through to a direct and primitive response of eye and ear. I know little of such matters, but there seems to me to be a gap between education and one important aspect of contemporary culture, and of imaginative power in general, that educational theory and practice have not to my knowledge yet bridged.

I spoke at the beginning of a tertiary phase of education. This phase, which is considerably more of an ideal than a fact, is symbolized, and perhaps occasionally achieved, by the liberal-arts program in the university, and by the four-year withdrawal from ordinary society which is devoted to it. Here the consolidating and exploring aspects of the mind take on still another relationship. The conservative aspect is now the awareness of the society that the student is living in, the knowledge of its institutions, conventions, and attitudes which enables him to take his rightful place in it. This is the end of all that aspect of education covered by such terms as "preparation for life" or "adjustment" to it. Over against this, in the ideally educated mind, is the awareness that the middle-class mid-twentieth century North American society we are living in is not the real form of human society, but the transient appearance of that society. The real human society is the total body of human achievement in the arts and sciences. The arts are perhaps more concerned with what humanity has done, the sciences perhaps more concerned with what it is about to do, but the two together form the permanent model of civilization which our present society approximates. This model is our cultural environment, as distinct from our social environment. The educated man is the man who tries to live in his social environment according to the standards of his cultural environment. This gives him some detachment about his own society, some understanding of the forces that make it change so rapidly, and some ability to distinguish its temporary expedients from its permanent values. It is unnecessary to labor the point that an age as revolutionary as ours, in which we have to adjust quickly and constantly to radical changes or disappear from history, needs such elements in its education.

In this final phase the imagination moves over to the exploring or radical side of the mind, and comes into its own. It is now a fully developed constructive power: It is informed by what Whitehead calls the habitual vision of greatness, and its activity in the world around it is to realize whatever it can of that vision. It operates in society in much the same way, working from conception to realization, that the artist works on his art, which is what Blake meant by saying that the poetic genius of man is the real man. The immediate purpose of teaching literature to children and adolescents is not to persuade them to appreciate or admire works of literature more, but to understand them with a critical intelligence blended of sympathy and detachment. Detachment without sympathy is Philistinism; sympathy without detachment is accurately called uncritical. But the ultimate purpose of teaching literature is not understanding, but the transferring of the imaginative habit of mind, the instinct to create a new form instead of idolizing an old one, from the laboratory of literature to the life of mankind. Society depends heavily for its well-being on the handful of people who are imaginative in this sense. If the number became a majority, we should be living in a very different world, for it would be the world that we should then have the vision and the power to construct.

NOTES

Notes

INSISTENT TASKS IN LANGUAGE LEARNING

1. Nelson Brooks, *Language and Language Learning* (New York: Harcourt, Brace, 1960), p. 43.

2. Modern Language Association of America, "An Articulated English Program: A Hypothesis to Test," *PMLA,* vol. 74, no. 4, pt. 2 (1959), pp. 13–19.

3. A. F. Watt, *Language and Mental Development of Children* (London: Harrap, 1944), p. 89.

4. E. L. Black, "The Difficulties of Training College Students in Understanding What They Read," *British Journal of Educational Psychology,* 24:17–30 (1954).

5. Melvin Roman, *Reaching Delinquents through Reading* (Springfield, Ill.: Charles C. Thomas, 1957), chap. ii; Helen M. Robinson, *Why Pupils Fail in Reading* (Chicago: University of Chicago Press, 1946), chap. vii.

6. C. P. Snow, *The Two Cultures and the Scientific Revolution* (New York: Cambridge University Press, 1961), p. 19.

7. A. N. Whitehead, *The Aims of Education* (London: Secker and Warburg, 1932), chap. i.

8. William James, *Talks to Teachers on Psychology and to Students on Some of Life's Ideals* (New York: Henry Holt, 1899), pp. 217–218.

9. Dorothea McCarthy, "Language Development in Children," *Manual of Child Psychology,* ed. L. Carmichael, 2nd ed. (New York: Wiley, 1954), pp. 492–630.

10. D. O. Hebb, "Drives and the C.N.S.," *Psychological Review,* 62:243–254 (1955).

11. C. M. Gibson and I. A. Richards, *First Steps in Reading English* (New York: Pocket Books, 1957). A full range of instructional material has also been developed by Language Research, Inc.

12. A. R. MacKinnon, *How Do Children Learn to Read?* (Toronto: Copp Clark, 1959).

13. *Ibid.,* chap. vii.

14. William Cory, "What a Schoolmaster Thought," *Essays of William Cory* (Oxford, 1897).

15. MacKinnon, pp. 163–177.

16. L. J. Cronbach, "Educational Psychology," *Annual Review of Psychology,* 1:235–254 (1950).

17. J. S. Bruner, *The Process of Education* (Cambridge, Mass.: Harvard University Press, 1960).

THE INGLIS LECTURES

THE BURTON LECTURES

1955 Hollis L. Caswell. *How Firm a Foundation? An Appraisal of Threats to the Quality of Elementary Education.*

1956 William S. Gray. *The Teaching of Reading: An International View.*

1957 George Dearborn Spindler. *The Transmission of American Culture.*

1958 Lawrence K. Frank. *The School as Agent for Cultural Renewal.*

THE INGLIS AND BURTON LECTURES

1960 Thomas Munro and Herbert Read. *The Creative Arts in American Education.*

1961 Joseph J. Schwab and Paul F. Brandwein. *The Teaching of Science.*

1962 Northrop Frye and A. R. MacKinnon. *Learning in Language and Literature.*